12/19

D0906797

Dallas
MAVERICKS

BY K.C. KELLEY

Published by The Child's World®
1980 Lookout Drive • Mankato, MN 56003-1705
800-599-READ • www.childsworld.com

Cover: © AP Images/Matt York.
Photographs ©: AP Images: Reed Saxon 9; CalSport Media 17; David
Plukip 18; Bob Galbraith 22; David Breslauer 29. Imagn/USA Today
Sports: Jerome Miron 6; Austin McAfee 10; Matthew Emmons 13; Kevin
Jairaj 25, 26; Jalen Brunson 26; Eric Harline 26. Newscom: Jeff Siner/TNS
5; Paul Moseley/TNS; Brian Rothmuller/Icon SW 26.

ISBN 9781503824652
LCCN 2018964197

Printed in the United States of America
PA02416

ABOUT THE AUTHOR

K.C. Kelley is a huge sports fan who has written more than 150 books for kids. He has written about football, basketball, soccer, and even auto racing! He lives in Santa Barbara, California.

TABLE OF

CONTENTS

GO, MAVERICKS!

The Dallas Mavericks headed into a new **era** in 2019. For nearly 21 seasons, their team was led by star Dirk Nowitzki. He retired after the 2018–19 season. Who would take over? Dallas fans will look for new heroes to lead their team. The Mavericks have been a top team for a long time. Will that continue? Let's meet the Mavericks!

Teenage star Luka Doncic led the Mavericaks in 2019.

It's a battle of Texas when the Houston Rockets (red) take on the Mavericks.

6

WHO ARE THE MAVERICKS?

The Mavericks are one of 30 NBA teams. The Mavericks play in the Southwest Division of the Western Conference. The other Southwest Division teams are the Houston Rockets, the Memphis Grizzlies, the New Orleans Pelicans, and the San Antonio Spurs. The Mavericks are big **rivals** with the Spurs and Rockets. All three teams play in Texas.

WHERE THEY CAME FROM

The Mavericks joined the NBA as an **expansion team** in 1980. The team gots its name from cowboy slang. A horse without a brand on it is called a maverick. That word later came to describe a person who is very independent. Many fans just call their team the Mavs for short.

James Donaldson of the Mavericks battles superstar Kareem Abdul-Jabbar in the 1988 Western Conference finals.

DeAndre Jordan leaped above the Atlanta Hawks of the Eastern Conference in this 2019 game.

WHO THEY PLAY

The Mavericks play 82 games each season. They play 41 games at home and 41 on the road. The Mavs play four games against each of the other Southwest Division teams. They play 36 games against other Western Conference teams. The Mavericks also play each of the teams in the Eastern Conference twice. That's a lot of basketball! Each June, the winners of the Western and Eastern Conferences play each other in the **NBA Finals**.

WHERE THEY PLAY

The Mavericks are one of two NBA teams that play in arenas named for American Airlines. The Miami Heat is the other. Dallas's American Airlines Center opened in 2001. It is also home to the Dallas Stars pro hockey team. When the Mavs play, fans get help cheering from two team **mascots**. MavsMan does great **slam dunks**. Champ is a blue-headed horse.

The Mavericks warmed up on the American Airlines Center court before a game. During a game, mascot Champ (left) helps the fans cheer.

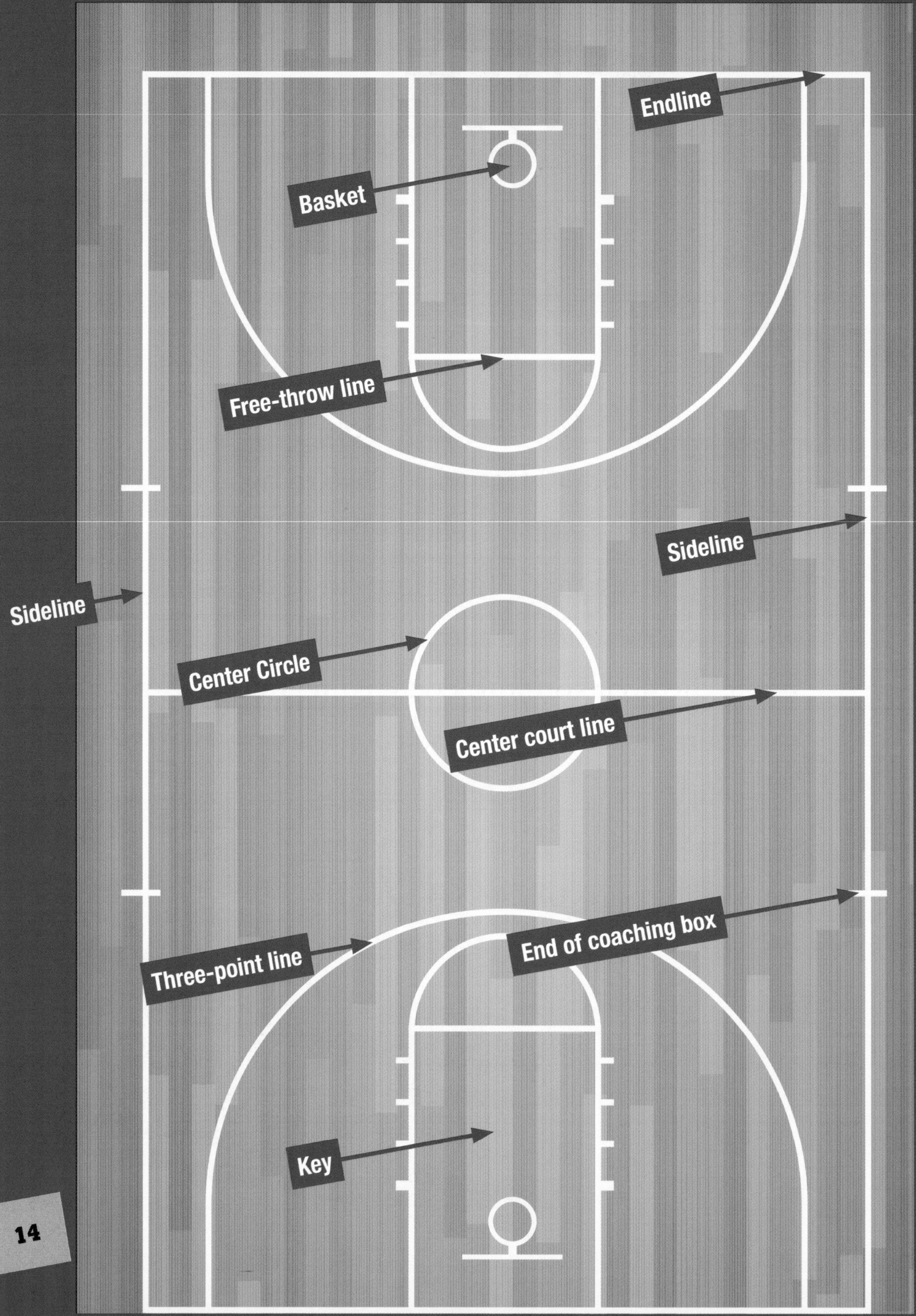

Endline

Basket

Free-throw line

Sideline

Sideline

Center Circle

Center court line

Three-point line

End of coaching box

Key

THE BASKETBALL COURT

An NBA court is 94 feet long and 50 feet wide (28.6 m by 15.24 m). Nearly all the courts are made from hard maple wood. Rubber mats under the wood help make the floor springy. Each team paints the court with its **logo** and colors. Lines on the court show the players where to take shots. The diagram on the left shows the important parts of the NBA court.

How does a basketball court become a hockey **rink**? Workers remove the wood panels. They spray water onto cold pipes. The water freezes, and machines smooth out the ice. Game on!

GOOD TIMES

Since 2000, the Mavericks have usually made the playoffs. Superstar Dirk Nowitzki led the way to the team's best seasons. In 2006, Dallas also won the Western Conference, but lost in the NBA Finals to the Miami Heat. In 2011, the Mavs won 57 games and the Southwest Division title. They played the Heat again in the Finals. That time, Dallas won the NBA championship!

Dirk Nowitzki proudly poses with the 2011 NBA championship trophy.

Not even a hand in the face by the Mavericks stopped this shot by Charlotte's Muggsy Bogues in a tough 1993 season.

TOUGH TIMES

The 1992–93 season for Dallas was pretty bad. The Mavs lost a team-record 71 games. They finished in last place in the Southwest Division. In one game that year, the Sacramento Kings scored 58 points more than the Mavs. It was the worst loss in team history! In 2017–18, Dallas also had a down year. The team won only 24 games.

ALL THE RIGHT MOVES

Dirk Nowitzki came to Dallas in 2000 with a powerful weapon. He used a fadeaway jumper. To make this shot, he leaned back as he jumped. Then he pushed the ball at the basket. No one could block this shot! Nowitzki ended his great career in 2019. He was sixth all-time in the NBA in points.

You can't stop this shot! Nowitzki shows how he leaned back to shoot his fadeaway.

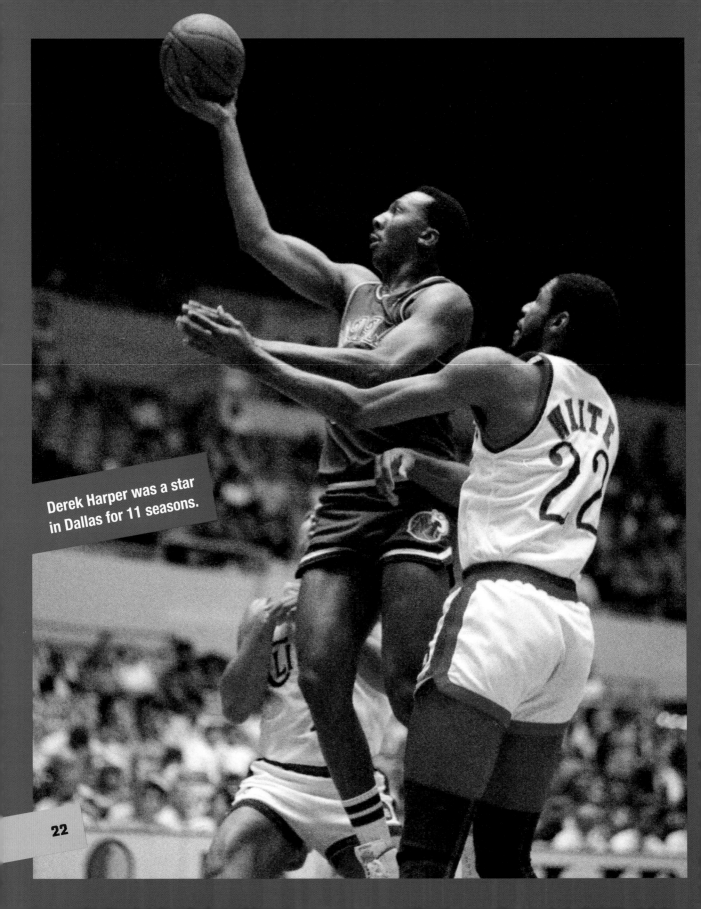

Derek Harper was a star in Dallas for 11 seasons.

HEROES THEN

Dallas had other stars before Dirk Nowitzki. In the team's early years, Rolando Blackman was an all-around star. He was named to four **All-Star Games**. Guard Derek Harper was the top player in Dallas in the early 1990s. Nowitzki joined the team in 1999 from Germany. Tall and talented, he became a superstar. He was the 2007 NBA Most Valuable Player. He was named to 14 All-Star teams. Nowitzki scored more points than any other player in Dallas history!

HEROES NOW

Like Dirk Nowitzki, Luka Doncic is a top player from Europe. Doncic was a star in Slovenia before joining the NBA. He combines great shooting with outstanding passing skills. Some of those passes go to Tim Hardaway Jr., a solid shooter. Another young star for Dallas is Harrison Barnes. Barnes moves quickly with the ball and is hard to **defend**.

Luka Doncic became an NBA All-Star in his first season, 2018–19.

25

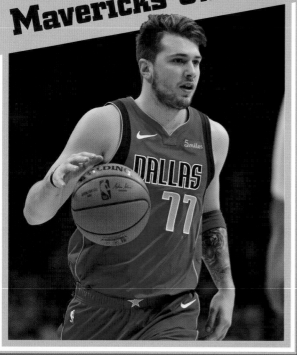

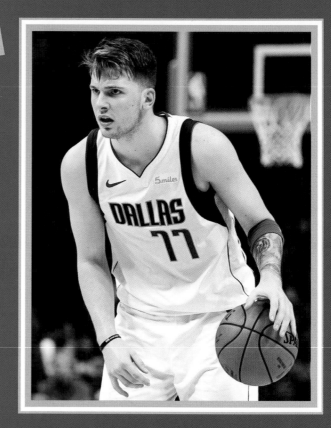

WHAT THEY WEAR

NBA players wear a **tank top** jersey. Players wear team shorts. Each player can choose his own sneakers. Some players also wear knee pads or wrist guards.

Each NBA team has more than one jersey style. The pictures at left show some of the Mavericks' jerseys.

The NBA basketball is 29.5 inches (75 cm) around. It is covered with leather. The leather has small bumps called pebbles.

The pebbles on a basketball help players grip it.

TEAM STATS

H ere are some of the all-time career records for the Dallas Mavericks. These stats are complete through all of the 2018–19 NBA regular season.

GAMES	
Dirk Nowitzki	1,522
Brad Davis	883

THREE-POINTERS	
Dirk Nowtizki	1,982
Jason Terry	1,140

ASSISTS PER GAME	
Jason Kidd	8.4
Steve Nash	7.2

REBOUNDS PER GAME	
Tyson Chandler	10.4
Roy Tarpley	10.0

STEALS PER GAME	
Jason Kidd	1.9
Fat Lever	1.8

FREE-THROW PCT.	
Steve Nash	.896
Darren Collison	.880

POINTS	
Dirk Nowitzki	31,560
Rolando Blackman	16,643

29

ROLANDO BLACKMAN

All-Star Games *(ALL-STAR GAYMZ)* events at which top players make teams to play each other.

defend *(dee-FEND)* try to prevent from scoring

era *(AIR-uh)* a period of time in history

expansion team *(ex-PAN-shun TEEM)* in sports, a team that is added to an existing league

mascot *(MASS-kot)* a costumed character that helps fans cheer

NBA Finals *(NBA FINE-ulz)* the championship series for the NBA

rebounder *(REE-bownd-er)* a player who grabs missed shots

rink *(RINK)* an oval-shaped sheet of ice used for hockey or skating

rivals *(RY-vuhlz)* two people or groups competing for the same thing

slam dunks *(SLAM DUNKS)* shots that are stuffed by one or two hands into the basket

tank top *(TANK TOP)* a style of shirt that has straps over the shoulders and no sleeves

FIND OUT MORE

IN THE LIBRARY

Goodman, Michael E. *NBA Champions: Dallas Mavericks.*
Mankato, MN: Creative Paperbacks, 2018.

Sports Illustrated Kids (editors). *Big Book of Who:*
Basketball. New York, NY: Sports Illustrated Kids, 2015.

Whiting, Jim. *The NBA: A History of Hoops: Dallas*
Mavericks. Mankato, MN: Creative Paperbacks, 2017.

ON THE WEB

Visit our website for links about the Dallas Mavericks:
childsworld.com/links

Note to Parents, Teachers, and Librarians: We routinely verify our Web links to make sure
they are safe and active sites. So encourage your readers to check them out!

INDEX